500 + Random Bits Of

USELESS TRIVIA

EMMA FOX

1

1 in every 5,000 babies
is born with a tooth.

2

23% of all photocopier faults worldwide
are caused by people sitting on them and
photocopying their buttocks.

3

35% of the people who use
personal ads for dating are
already married.

4

8% of the human DNA is viral in origin.

5

85% of plant life is found in the ocean.

6

A baby spider is called a "spiderling".

7

A bear has 42 teeth (most adult humans have 32 permanent teeth.

8

A cat can jump up to six times its body length in one leap.

9

Baby names must be approved by the local registration office in Germany.

10

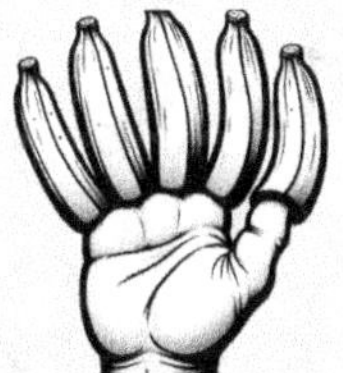

a cluster of bananas is called a "hand"; a single banana is a "finger".

11

A cow gives nearly 200,000 glasses of milk in her lifetime.

12

A cow-bison hybrid is called a "beefalo."

13

"Antidisestablishmentarianism" is one of the longest non-technical and non-coined words in the English language.

14

A day on Mercury lasts approximately as long as 59 days on Earth.

15

A day on Venus is longer than a year on Venus. It takes Venus longer to rotate once on its axis than to complete one orbit of the Sun.

16

A dragonfly has a lifespan of 24 hours.

17

A duck's quack doesn't echo. No one knows why.

18

A duel between three people is actually called a "truel".

19

A giraffe can clean its own ears with its 21-inch tongue.

20

A goldfish has a memory span of three seconds.

21

A group of crows is called a "murder".

22

A group of flamingos is known as a "flamboyance" and also as a "stand".

23

Rubber bands last longer when refrigerated.

24

A group of kangaroos is called a "mob".

25

A group of owls is called a "parliament".

26

A group of pugs is
called a "grumble".

27

Apple seeds contain cyanide.

28

A group of twelve or more cows is
called a "flink".

29

A group of unicorns is called a "blessing".

30

A hummingbird weighs less than a penny.

31

A lobsters blood is colorless but when exposed to oxygen it turns blue.

32

A narwhal's tusk reveals its health condition.

33

A raisin dropped in a glass of fresh champagne will bounce up and down continuously from the bottom of the glass to the top.

34

A rhinoceros horn is made of compacted hair.

35

A shrimp's heart is in its head, located in the thorax which fuses with the head.

36

A single cloud can weigh more than 1 MILLION pounds!

37

A single strand of spaghetti is called a "spaghetto".

38

A ten-gallon hat will only hold ¾ of a gallon.

39

The seahorse is the only fish that swims with an upright posture, giving it a unique appearance.

40

A toaster uses almost half as much energy as a full-sized oven.

41

About 11% of people
are left-handed.

42

Alligators will give
manatees the right of way
if they encounter each
other in the wild.

43

Almonds are a member of
the peach family.

44

It is physically impossible for
pigs to look up into the sky
(unless they are lying on their
backs).

45

An adult human has fewer bones than a baby. Babies have more bones than adults, with 270 bones at birth that fuse into 206–213 bones in adulthood.

46

Bamboo is the fastest growing plant in the world.

47

An eagle can kill a young deer and fly away with it.

48

An octopus has three hearts and nine brains, one central brain and eight smaller brains controlling each arm.

49

Sloths can hold their breath longer than dolphins.

50

"allodoxaphobia" is the fear of other people's opinions. People with allodoxaphobia may experience constant anxiety when hearing what others think about them.

51

Armadillos are the only animal besides humans that can get leprosy.

52

Astronauts are not allowed to eat beans before they go into space because passing wind in a spacesuit damages them.

53

August has the highest percentage of births.

54

Bananas are curved because they grow towards the sun due to a process called "negative geotropism". This means that instead of growing towards the ground, bananas turn towards the sun to retrieve light.

55

Bananas are slightly radioactive due to the presence of potassium-40, a radioactive isotope of potassium.

56

Because metal was scarce, the Oscars given out during World War II were made of wood.

57

Bees can recognize human faces using a mechanism similar to how humans recognize faces.

58

Bees sometimes sting other bees. Bees use their stingers for self-defense, such as when defending their nests from intruders. For example, bees may mistake other bees for intruders and accidentally sting them.

59

Before 1913, some parents managed to mail their kids to Grandma's – through the postal service.

60

High heels were originally designed for men and appeared in Persia in the 10th century.

61

Male Billy Goats smell so bad because they urinate on their own head, beard, and front legs to smell more attractive to females during their mating season.

62

Birds rely on gravity to swallow because their esophageal muscles do not contract strongly enough to propel food down.

63

Japan has around 5,520,000 vending machines, which equates to one vending machine for every 23 persons.

64

BOOKKEEPER and BOOKKEEPING are the only words in the English language with three consecutive double letters.

65

Bruce Lee was so fast that they actually had to slow film down so you could see his moves.

66

Bubble wrap was originally intended to be used as wallpaper and was invented in 1957 before becoming popular as packing material.

67

Buttered toast frequently falls butter-side down due to the way it rotates as it falls, which is caused by air pockets in the bread and the height of the table.

68

Camels have three eyelids to protect themselves from blowing sand.

69

Cap'n Crunch's full name is Horatio Magellan Crunch.

70

Most cats have 5 toes on the front paws and 4 on the back paws. If a cat has 6 toes, they have a genetic condition called "polydactyly".

71

Cats have over one hundred vocal sounds, while dogs only have about ten.

72

Chewing gum while peeling onions will keep you from crying.

73

Cleopatra lived closer in time to the moon landing than to the construction of the Great Pyramid of Giza.

74

Cookie Monster's real name is "Sid". He revealed his name in a song in 2004.

75

Dogs have three eyelids. Located at the inside corner of the eye, the third eyelid protects the surface of the eye.

76

Dolphins have been trained to be used in wars.

77

Dolphins sleep with one eye open.

78

In the 16th century, it was common for European nobles to keep pet bears as a status symbol, even bringing them to parties. Badgers, weasels, ferrets, squirrels and even monkeys made for popular pets as well.

79

Dreamt is the only English word that ends in the letters "mt".

80

Duffel bags are named after a town in Flanders, Belgium. According to the Oxford English Dictionary, the word dates back to 1649, used to describe 'a coarse woollen cloth having a thick nap or frieze'.

81

During your lifetime, you will produce enough saliva to fill two swimming pools.

82

The official state gem of Washington is petrified wood.

83

Each king in a deck of playing cards represents a great king from history: Spades - King David; Hearts - Charlemagne; Clubs -Alexander, the Great; Diamonds - Julius Caesar.

84

Each time you see a full moon you always see the same side.

85

Earth is the only planet not named after a god.

86

Elephants are the only animals that can't jump.

87

Every continent has a city called "Rome" except Antarctica.

88

Fear of the number 13 is called "triskaidekaphobia" (truh·skai·deh·kuh·fow·bee·uh).

89

Febreze was originally marketed as a way to remove cigarette smoke from fabric.

90

Firehouses have circular stairways because of the horses that used to pull the fire trucks. The horses would follow the smell of food and climb the stairs, so the firemen installed spiral staircases to prevent this.

91

Following a 2011 ban, it is illegal in France to sell dolls that do not have human faces. This means that if dolls have human bodies, their faces must also be easily recognized as humans.

92

France was still executing people by guillotine when the first Star Wars movie was released in 1977.

93

French poodles actually originated in Germany.

94

Frogs can't vomit. If one absolutely has to, it will vomit its entire stomach.

95

Giant squids have the largest eyes in the animal kingdom.

96

Gorillas burp when they are happy.

97

Humans are the only animals that blush.

98

Honeybees can recognize human faces, which they see as a "strange flower".

99

Horses can't vomit.

100

When the word "helicopter" is broken down into prefix and suffix, it is "helico" and "pter" rather than "heli" and "copter". Helico stands for spiral, and pter for wing.

101

If you could fold a piece of paper 42 times, it would reach to the moon.

102

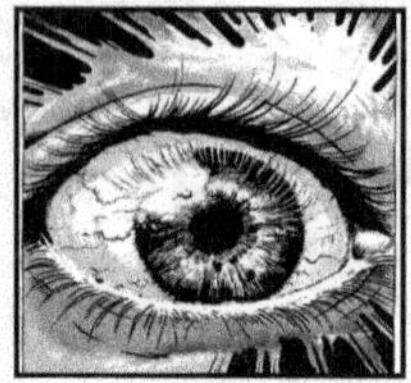

If you keep your eyes open by force when you sneeze, you might pop an eyeball out.

103

If you lift a kangaroo's tail off the ground it can't hop, because it needs its tail for balance.

104

If you sneeze too hard, you can fracture a rib. If you try to suppress a sneeze, you can rupture a blood vessel in your head or neck and die.

105

A hurricane releases more energy in 10 minutes than all the world's nuclear weapons.

106

If you stop getting thirsty, you need to drink more water. When a human body is dehydrated, its thirst mechanism shuts off.

107

Every time you lick a stamp, you consume 1/10 of a calorie.

108

In 1923, jockey Frank Hayes won a race at Belmont Park in New York despite being dead—he suffered a heart attack mid-race, but his body stayed in the saddle until his horse crossed the line for a 20–1 outsider victory.

109

Between 2011 - 2017, more people were killed from injuries caused by taking a selfie than by shark attacks.

110

In ancient Egypt, priests plucked every hair from their bodies, including their eyebrows and eyelashes. They believed hair was unclean.

111

In ancient Greek, the word "idiot" originally meant someone who didn't participate in public life or politics.

112

In ancient Rome, lemons were used as an antidote to several poisons.

113

In Ancient Rome, "unclean bread" made from wheat and mixed with chalk was sold in the marketplaces.

114

Humans share 50% of their DNA with bananas.

115

New Jersey is the world's top producer of eggplants, harvesting 849 acres annually, which is more than any other state.

116

In France, it is legal to marry a dead person.

117

In Japan, letting a sumo wrestler make your baby cry is considered good luck.

118

In most advertisements, the time displayed on a watch is 10:10 because it's considered aesthetically pleasing..

119

In some parts of the world, rats are considered a delicacy, including Cambodia, Laos, Myanmar, parts of the Philippines and Indonesia, Thailand, Ghana, China, and Vietnam.

120

In 2011, more than 1 in 3 divorce filings in the U.S. contained the word 'Facebook'.

121

Barbie's full name is Barbara Millicent Roberts. Barbie is a fictional character created by Ruth Handler, co-founder of Mattel Inc., in 1959.

122

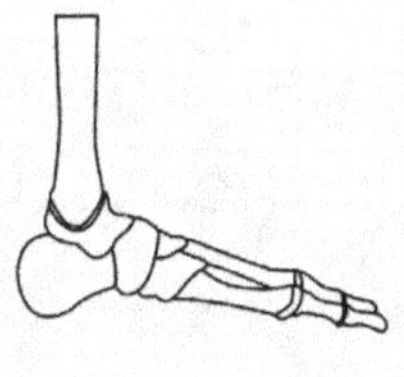

One quarter of the bones in your body are in your feet. Each foot contains 26 bones, which is about 25.24% of the total bone count in the body.

123

It's estimated that Americans eat 50 billion hamburgers each year.

124

In Uganda, around 48% of the population is under 15 years of age.

125

In Utah, it's illegal to swear in front of a dead person as defiling a dead body is a third-degree felony

126

Intelligent people have more zinc and copper in their hair.

127

Close to 70 percent of the world's freshwater is held in glaciers and ice sheets.

128

The only domestic animal not mentioned in the Bible is the cat.

129

Apples are more effective at waking you up in the morning than coffee.

130

It is impossible for most people to lick their own elbow.

131

Almost everyone that reads this will try to lick their elbow.

132

It rains diamonds on Jupiter and Saturn.

133

It takes a photon, on average, 170,000 years to travel from the core of the sun to the surface.

134

It's illegal to sell a "haunted" house in New York without telling the buyer.

135

It's against the law to burp or sneeze in a church in Nebraska, USA.

136

It's illegal to own a single goldfish in Switzerland for its well being.

137

The longest recorded flight of a chicken is 13 seconds.

138

It is illegal in Alaska to wake a sleeping bear to take a photo.

139

It's impossible to sneeze with your eyes open.

140

It's possible to turn peanut butter into diamonds through a process that uses heat and pressure.

141

King Henry Eighth slept with a gigantic axe beside him.

142

Koalas have fingerprints almost identical to humans.

143

Lemons contain more sugar than strawberries. A lemon contains 70% sugar and a strawberry contains only 40% of sugar.

144

Leonardo Da Vinci invented scissors. Also, it took him 12 years to paint Mona Lisa's lips.

145

Los Angeles's full name is "El Pueblo de Nuestra Senora la Reina de los Angeles de Porciuncula" and can be abbreviated to 3.63% of its size, "L.A."

146

Maine is the only state (in USA) whose name is just one syllable.

147

Mice sing like birds but humans can't hear them.

148

More human twins are being born now than ever before.

149

More Monopoly money is printed in a year than real money printed around the world.

150

More people are allergic to cow's milk than any other food.

151

Maine is the only state to border exactly one other American state (New Hampshire).

152

Most dust particles in your house are made from dead skin.

153

New York drifts about one inch farther away from London each year.

154

New Zealanders have more pets per household than any other country.

155

No piece of square dry paper can be folded more than seven times in half.

156

No word in the English language rhymes with month, orange, silver, or purple.

157

Octopuses lay 56,000 eggs at a time.

158

On average, 12 newborns will be given to the wrong parents daily.

159

The average person's left hand does 56% of the typing.

160

Oxford University is older than the Aztec Empire. Oxford University had already been established for several centuries before the Aztec Empire was founded in 1325.

161

One in every five adults believes that aliens are hiding on our planet disguised as humans.

162

One of the ingredients in dynamite is peanuts.

163

1 Million SECONDS = 11 DAYS.

164

Our eyes are always the same size from birth, but our nose and ears never stop growing.

165

Penguins propose to their mates with a pebble.

166

Trained Pigeons can tell the difference between a painting by Monet and Picasso.

167

Polar bears could eat as many as 86 penguins in a single sitting.

168

Rabbits cannot vomit. Rabbits have a strong sphincter that keeps stomach juice from entering the esophagus, and their sensitive stomach muscles and weak diaphragm can't push food back up the throat.

169

Rabbits like licorice root, but it can be bad for them because they can't digest sugars.

170

Ralph Lauren's original name is "Ralph Lifshitz".

171

A leap year isn't always every four years. While most leap years occur every four years, there is an exception to the rule. If the year can be evenly divided by 100 but not 400, it is not a leap year. For example, the year 1900 was not a leap year, but 2000 was.

172

Rats laugh when tickled.

173

Finland has the world's greatest concentration of heavy metal bands, with approximately 70.6 bands per 100,000 people.

174

Recycling one glass bottle saves enough energy to watch TV for 20 minutes.

175

Reindeer like bananas.

176

Rubik's cubes have over 43 quintillion possible combinations.

177

Candy corn was originally known as "Chicken Feed". Production started in the late 1880s.

178

Scotland has 421 words for "snow."

179

The longest English palindrome is "tattarrattat" at 12 letters long.

180

Sea otters hold hands when they sleep so they don't drift away from each other.

181

Honey bees have microscopic hairs on their two bigger eyes, which are thought to help them navigate in windy weather. The hairs may also assist bees collect and protect pollen.

182

An ostrich's eye is bigger than its brain.

183

Some worms will eat themselves if they can't find any food.

184

"Sphenopalatine ganglioneuralgia" is the scientific term for brain freeze.

185

Starfish don't have a brain or blood! In fact, they employ purified sea water to transport nutrients via their nervous system.

186

Termites outweigh humans by almost ten to one. For every person on Earth, there are 1,000 pounds of termites.

187

The "sixth sick sheik's sixth sheep's sick" is said to be the toughest tongue twister in the English language.

188

The "W" in Morse Code is dot-dash-dash.

• – –

189

The average person falls asleep in seven minutes.

190

The average person laughs 10 times a day.

191

The average person walks the equivalent of five times around the world in their lifetime.

192

Dentistry is one of the oldest professions in the world. Evidence of teeth being drilled into dates back to 9,000 years.

193

"Harry Potter and the Deathly Hallows" is the fastest selling book in history.

194

The chainsaw was originally created to aid in childbirth.

195

The characters Bert and Ernie on Sesame Street were named after Bert the cop and Ernie the taxi driver in Frank Capra's "It's a Wonderful Life."

196

In 1823, Johann Wolfgang Döbereiner, a German chemist, created the first lighter called "Döbereiner's lamp", which generated a flame using hydrogen gas and a platinum catalyst. The modern friction match, however, was developed a few years later in 1826 by English chemist John Walker.

197

Only one person in two billion will live to be 116 or older.

198

Snakes smell with their tongue.

199

The first CD pressed in the US was Bruce Springsteen's "Born in the USA."

200

The first computer "bug" was identified in 1947 as a dead moth stuck in a Harvard computer.

201

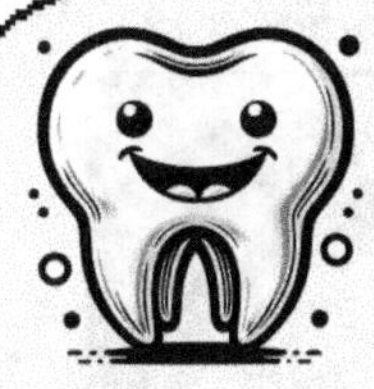

Human teeth are the only part of the body that cannot heal themselves.

202

The first footprints on the moon will remain there for a million years. Unlike on Earth, there is no air or water movement to erode or wash away the footprints.

203

The first item ever sold on eBay was a broken laser pointer.

204

The first oranges weren't orange — they were green.

205

The first soft drink in space was Coca-Cola in 1985.

206

The first sales pitch for the Nerf ball was "Nerf: You can't hurt babies or old people!"

207

The first product to have a barcode was Wrigley's gum scanned at retail checkout on June 26, 1974.

208

The first telephone call ever made was by Alexander Graham Bell, saying "Mr. Watson, come here, I want to see you.'

209

The founder of Match.com lost his girlfriend to a man she met on Match.com.

210

The Goodyear Blimp is the official bird of Redondo Beach, California.

211

The Guinness Book of Records holds the record for being the book most often stolen from Public Libraries.

212

The Hawaiian alphabet has only 12 letters. There are five vowels: A, E, I, O, and U. There are also seven consonants: H, K, L, M, N, P, and W.

213

The heart of a blue whale is as large as a small car.

214

The Eiffel Tower is repainted every seven years, requiring about 60 tons of paint each time.

215

The inventor of the microwave appliance, Percy Spencer, only received $2 for his discovery.

216

The inventor of the umbrella was originally going to call it the "brella'. "Um" was added later for clarity.

217

The inventor of the Waffle Iron did not like waffles. Cornelius Swartwout was an American inventor who patented his waffle iron on August 24, 1869.

218

The last letter added to the English alphabet wasn't 'Z', it was the letter 'J'.

219

The least used letter in the alphabet is 'Z'. 'Q' is the second least commonly used.

220

The longest hiccuping spree: Charles Osborne hiccupped continuously for 68 years, from 1922 to 1990.

221

The longest English word
without a vowel is "rhythms."

222

The longest muscle in your body is the sartorius.
It runs from the hip to the knee, and can be up to
600 mm long. The word "sartor" signifies tailor
in Latin. It is frequently referred to as the "tailor's
muscle" due to its ability to aid in actions that
need us to sit cross-legged. That is the stance
that tailors have previously used to work.

223

One of the longest one-syllable
word in the English language is
"screeched."

224

The longest place name on the planet is 85
characters long and located in New Zealand:
"Taumatawhakatangihangakoauauotamateaturipu
kakapikimaungahoronukupokaiwhenuakitanatahu".

225

The longest wedding veil was the same length as 63.5 football fields.

226

The majority of the world's oxygen is produced by the ocean.

227

The majority of your brain is fat.

228

The medical name for a butt crack is "intergluteal cleft."

229

Percy Spencer is credited with creating microwave cooking after observing a chocolate bar melted in his pocket while investigating radar in 1945.

230

The most commonly used letter in the alphabet is "E'. It appears in about 11% of the words in the dictionary.

231

The oldest "your mom" joke was discovered on a 3,500 year old Babylonian tablet.

232

The only continent with no active volcanoes is Australia.

233

The only letters that do not appear on the periodic table are "J" and "Q".

234

Some people used to think forks were sacrilegious, immoral, unsanitary, and even a devil's tool.

235

The original London Bridge is now in Lake Havasu City, Arizona. In 1968, it was purchased from the City of London by Robert P. McCulloch.

236

The original name for basketball, as invented by Dr. James Naismith in 1891, was "Basket Ball." Two peach baskets and a soccer ball were used.

237

The original name for butterfly was flutterby.

238

The original name for the hashtag symbol is "octothorpe", derived from the prefix octo-, which signifies the eight points on the symbol, and "Thorpe", which potentially originates from the Old English meaning for "village".

239

The placement of a donkey's eyes in its head enables it to see all four feet at all times.

240

The king of hearts is the only king without a mustache in a standard deck of playing cards.

241

The shortest complete sentence in English is "I am."

242

The shortest place name is "Å" and it's located in both Sweden and Norway. It means "stream" or "river" in Scandinavian languages.

243

The first Frisbees were pie plates or cookie tin lids made by Frisbie Baking Company in Bridgeport, Connecticut.

244

The shortest war on record was fought between Britain and Zanzibar on August 27, 1896. Zanzibar surrendered after 45 minutes.

245

The six official languages of the United Nations are: English, French, Arabic, Chinese, Russian, and Spanish.

246

Australia is "technically" wider than the moon. The diameter of the Moon is 3400 kilometers, whereas the east-west diameter of Australia approaches 4000 kilometers.

247

The smallest bone in the human body is the stapes bone located in the ear; it is smaller than a grain of rice.

248

The space between your eyebrows is called the "glabella".

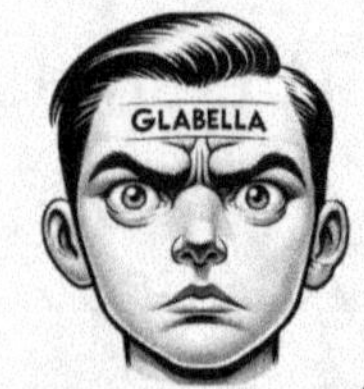

249

The state vegetable of Oklahoma is the watermelon, which is technically a fruit.

250

The strongest muscle in the human body is the masseter, one of the four muscles responsible for chewing.

251

The tongue is the only muscle in one's body that is attached from one end.

252

The total number of steps in the Eiffel Tower is 1,665. You can only climb 674 of them due to safety reasons.

253

There are approximately 2.5 million ants for every human on the planet.

254

The Twitter bird actually has a name, Larry the Bird, named after NBA legend Larry Bird.

255

The unicorn is the national animal of Scotland, a symbol of purity and strength in Celtic mythology.

256

The wood frog can hold its pee for up to eight months to survive winter.

257

The Alexander Piano is one of the world's largest pianos. Built by Adrian Mann, from New Zealand, who was 15 years old when he started to build it.

258

The world's largest yo-yo is 11 feet, 10.75 inches in diameter and weighs 4,620 pounds.

259

The Ljubljana Marshes Wheel, discovered in 2002 in the Ljubljana Marshes of Slovenia, is considered the world's oldest wooden wheel.

260

The world's quietest room is located at Microsoft's headquarters in Washington state.

261

The world's smallest park is two feet in diameter and located in Portland, Oregon. Mill Ends Park is a tiny urban park, consisting of one tree, located in the median strip of SW Naito Parkway.

262

The world's youngest parents were 8 and 9 and lived in China in 1910. The youngest mother was 5 years old.

263

The Sun is 93 million miles away, so sunlight takes 8 and 1/3 minutes to get to us.

264

There are more fake flamingos in the world than real ones.

265

There are no clocks in Las Vegas gambling casinos.

266

The most unpopular National Park is Gates of the Arctic National Park & Preserve. This massive park in Alaska lacks roads and paths. In 2023, it had just over 11,000 recreational visits, making it the least visited of the 63 national parks.

267

There are only four words in the English language which end in "dous": tremendous, horrendous, stupendous, and hazardous.

268

One billion seconds is 31 years.

269

There is a species of jellyfish, Turritopsis dohrnii, that is immortal, able to revert to its juvenile form after reaching adulthood.

270

There is no synonym for the word "thesaurus."

271

There's a basketball court on the top floor of the U.S. Supreme Court Building, known as the "Highest Court in the Land."

272

Cows have best friends and become stressed if they are separated. Just like humans, cows form close friendships and can experience stress when separated from their preferred companions.

273

Tigers have striped skin not just striped fur. The stripes are like fingerprints and no two tigers have the same pattern.

274

To escape the grip of a crocodile's jaw, push your thumb into its eyeballs-it will let you go instantly.

275

'Topolino" is the name for Mickey Mouse Italy.

276

Typewriter is the longest word that can be typed using only the top row of a standard QWERTY keyboard.

277

Unless food is mixed with saliva you can't taste it.

278

Vending machines kill more people each year than sharks do. The yearly risk in the U.S. of dying from a shark bite is roughly 1 in 250 million. In contrast, the yearly risk of dying from a vending machine accident is roughly 1 in 112 million.

279

Watermelons can keep you cool and hydrated as they are 92% water.

280

Wearing headphones for just an hour will increase the bacteria in your ear by 700 times.

281

When the moon is directly overhead, you will weigh slightly less.

282

Winston Churchill was born in 1874 in a ladies cloak room during a dance.

283

Wombat poop is cube-shaped and they can produce up to 100 per night.

284

The inside ingredients of a Kit Kat include the ground up layers of other Kit Kats.

285

You can't cry in space because your tears won't ever fall or to be exact you can cry but it would not be a pleasant experience.

286

White chocolate is technically not regarded "real" chocolate since it lacks cocoa solids. However, it does contain cocoa butter.

287

You can't breathe and swallow at the same time.

288

You can't hum while holding your nose closed because humming requires air movement.

289

Some ranch dressings are dyed with titanium dioxide to make them appear whiter.

290

Kings and Queens of England have two birthdays every year.

291

You replace every particle in your body every seven years. You are literally not the same person you were seven years ago.

292

Chimichanga means "thingamajig".

293

Your stomach has to produce a new layer of mucus every two weeks otherwise it will digest itself.

294

In 1614, Pocahontas was baptized and given the English name, "Rebecca".

295

There's a town in Pennsylvania named "Intercourse".

296

There are no public railways in Iceland.

297

There is an official World Rock Paper Scissors Association (WRPSA).

298

Victor Gruen, the man known as "father of the modern shopping mall," hated shopping.

299

The shortest commercial flight in the world is less than two minutes long, between two Scottish islands.

300

In Tennessee, it's illegal to catch a fish with a lasso. Tennessee code 70-4-104 forbids the use of all fishing equipment except for rod, reel and hook.

301

Airlines saved $40,000 in 1987 by eliminating one olive from each salad served in first class.

302

The voice actors of Mickey Mouse and Minnie Mouse got married in real life.

303

The word "girl" originally meant a young person of either sex; it was not specifically female.

304

Some people are more afraid of spiders than death.

305

February used to be the last month of the year in Roman times.

306

The house fly hums in the middle octave key of F.

307

Cows can walk upstairs but not downstairs.

308

There is a town in Nebraska called "Monowi" with a population of one. The only resident is also the mayor, bartender, and librarian.

309

The majority of the world's hazelnuts, about 70%, are used to make Nutella.

310

There's a single ATM in Antarctica.

311

A group of pandas is known as an "embarrassment".

312

Vatican City is the smallest country in the world by land area, covering just over 44 hectares (110 acres).

313

The Vatican City has the highest wine consumption per capita in the world.

314

The state of Florida is bigger than England. England is only .77 times as big as Florida.

315

It is illegal to step on money in Thailand. it is illegal to step on any of the Thai currency, the Baht. Why? Because the King's face is printed and engraved on the Thai notes and coins.

316

South Dakota is the only U.S state which shares no letters with the name of its capital, "Pierre".

317

You cannot bring a bear to the beach in Israel.

318

All British tanks since 1945 are equipped with tea making facilities.

319

A giraffe can go longer without water than a camel can.

320

Only two countries use purple in their national flags: Dominica and Nicaragua.

321

Yogurt originated in Turkey, and the origin of the word "yogurt" comes from the Turkish word yoğurt.

322

Four out of five children are able to recognize the McDonald's logo by the age of three.

323

The name for the shape of Pringles is called a "hyperbolic paraboloid'.

324

Before erasers were invented, breadcrumbs were used to erase mistakes.

325

In the 1830s, ketchup was used as medicine to treat such ailments as diarrhea, indigestion and jaundice.

326

The Japanese word "Komorebi" refers to sunlight filtering through trees. It's pronounced "koh-mo-reh-bee".

327

Newborns don't have kneecaps. Kneecaps don't completely develop until after six months.

328

The national anthem of Greece, "Hymn to Liberty", has 158 verses.

329

No president of the United States was an only child.

330

The world's oldest toy is a stick, and has been inducted into the Hall of Fame since 2008.

331

The word "gorilla" is derived from a Greek word meaning, "a tribe of hairy women."

332

The best place in the world to see rainbows is in Hawaii, the "Rainbow State".

333

In the UK, it's illegal to handle salmon in suspicious circumstances. This applies to anyone who receives or disposes of salmon in circumstances where they believe, or could reasonably believe, that the salmon has been illegally fished.

334

The number four is considered unlucky in many parts of East Asia because it sounds like the word for "death."

335

McDonald's once made bubblegum-flavored broccoli. This idea failed as it didn't taste good.

336

The shortest English word that contains the letters A, B, C, D, E, and F is "feedback."

337

You can hear a blue whale's heartbeat from more than 2 miles away.

338

The smell of freshly-cut grass is actually a plant distress call. Green leaf volatiles (GLVs), organic compounds released by damaged plants, are the source of the odor.

339

The original name for the search engine Google was "Backrub", because the search engine used backlinks to rank pages.

340

Each year, Americans buy 113 million cans of Spam. This means that 3.8 cans are eaten per second in the United States.

341

The official bird of Redondo Beach, California, is the Goodyear Blimp.

342

There's an opera house on the U.S.-Canada border where the stage is in one country and half the audience is in another. It is the Haskell Free Library and Opera House.

343

In 2005, a fortune cookie company correctly predicted the winning lottery number, resulting in 110 winners.

344

The plastic tips at the end of shoelaces are called "aglets".

345

In ancient Egypt, servants were smeared with honey to attract flies away from the pharaoh.

346

Ronald Reagan was a lifeguard during high school and saved 77 people's lives.

347

The inventor of the modern toilet was "Thomas Crapper".

348

The tongue is the strongest muscle in the human body relative to its size, capable of supporting significant weight and force.

349

New York was briefly named "New Orange" in 1673.

350

OKINOSHIMA is a tiny island in Japan that can only be visited by men, and they must be naked before they arrive to purify themselves.

351

More than 80% of the Earth's surface has never been mapped with the same detail as the moon.

352

Bees can fly higher than Mount Everest.

353

Sunglasses were originally designed for Chinese judges to hide their facial expressions in court.

354

A group of cats is called a "clowder"

355

Snails sleep for periods of 13 to 15 hours. Some hibernation-like periods can last years.

356

The coldest temperature ever recorded on Earth was -128.6 degrees Fahrenheit in Antarctica.

357

The first novel ever written on a typewriter was "Tom Sawyer."

358

The only part of the body that has no blood supply is the cornea of the eye. It receives oxygen directly from the air.

359

Every year, hundreds of new trees grow because of squirrels forgetting where they buried their nuts.

360

The French language has seventeen different words for "surrender."

361

The first product to be sold in an aerosol spray can was Dri-Sol marketed in 1941 as a disinfectant.

362

The first animated feature film made in the U.S. was Snow White and the Seven Dwarfs.

363

There's a volcano in Indonesia that spews blue lava, due to the high sulfur content.

364

The fastest gust of wind ever recorded on Earth was 253 miles per hour.

365

The original color of Coca-Cola
was green.

366

Charlie Chaplin once
won third prize in a
Charlie Chaplin look-
alike contest.

367

If every Oreo ever made were lined
up, it would reach the moon and
back five times.

368

The tiny pocket in jeans
was designed to store
pocket watches.

369

In 2021 three French men, Morgan Niquet, François Robin and Julien Serri, set the record for the most varieties of cheeses on a pizza. They used 834 different types of cheese!

370

Most American car horns honk in the key of "F".

371

Oxter is an old english word for "armpit".

372

The oldest "your mom" joke was discovered on a 3,500-year-old Babylonian tablet.

373

Only one in two billion people will live to be 116 or older.

374

In ancient Greece, throwing an apple at someone was considered a marriage proposal.

375

Sperm whales have the biggest brains of any animal on earth (more than 5 times heavier than a human brain).

376

The Eiffel Tower can grow more than six inches during the summer due to the expansion of the iron on hot days.

377

Bananas are berries, but strawberries are not.

378

More than 80% of the ocean is unexplored and unmapped.

379

Honey does not spoil. You could feasibly eat 3000-year-old honey.

380

Fish scales can be found in nail polish, lipstick, mascara, shampoo & conditioner, bath treatments, and scents. Guanine is a crystalline substance derived from crushed up fish scales that produces a shimmering look.

381

One single teaspoon of honey represents the life work of 12 bees.

382

The dot over the letter "i" and "j" is called a "tittle".

383

Salt was once used as a currency.

384

If you passed gas continuously for six years and nine months, you would generate enough gas to power an atomic weapon.

385

Catfish have over 27,000 taste buds. Humans have around 7,000.

386

Every "c" in Pacific Ocean is pronounced differently.

387

There is an island called "Just Enough Room Island". It islocated in Alexandria Bay, New York, and is just slightly larger than a tennis court.

388

The bird that can fly the longest distance without landing is the Alpine Swift, which can stay airborne for up to six months.

389

Butterflies taste
with their feet.

390

Buckingham Palace has a total of 775
rooms. These include 19 State rooms,
52 Royal and guest bedrooms, 188 staff
bedrooms, 92 offices and 78 bathrooms.

391

The highest grossing movie franchise is
Marvel Cinematic Universe.

392

Dolphins have
names for each
other.

393

President Abe Lincoln was a champion wrestler.

394

There are 18 different animal shapes in the Animal Crackers cookie zoo.

395

An octopus will eat its own arms if it gets really hungry.

396

For plumbers, the day after Thanksgiving is their busiest day of the year (mostly for stopped up sinks and garbage disposals).

397

Zippers were originally used for closing boots and tobacco pouches.

398

Penguins can leap up to 6 feet out of the water.

399

A baby octopus is about the size of a flea when it is born.

400

The world's deepest postbox is in Susami Bay in Japan. It's 10 meters underwater.

401

A snail can sleep for three years.

402

The shortest complete sentence in the English language is "Go."

403

On average, 100 people die by choking on ballpoint pens each year.

404

Animals that lay eggs don't have belly buttons. Belly buttons form where the umbilical cord connects. Creatures born from eggs never have an umbilical cord.

405

A group of rhinoceroses is called a "crash".

406

The banana tree is not a "tree', it is the world's largest herb.

407

The space suit worn by Neil Armstrong during the Apollo 11 mission was made by a bra manufacturer.

408

The first alarm clock could only ring at 4 a.m.

409

The largest recorded snowflake was 15 inches wide and 8 inches thick. It fell in Montana in 1887.

410

The original Monopoly game was circular.

411

Women hiccup less than men.

412

The longest time a person has ever been in full body contact with snow without any protective gear is 60 minutes.

413

The first potato chip flavor was salt and vinegar, created accidentally by the chef George Crum in 1853 when a customer complained that his fries were too thick and soggy.

414

Walter Morrison, the inventor of the frisbee was turned into a frisbee after he died.

415

It's illegal to carry an ice cream cone in your back pocket in Kentucky.

416

The world's largest padlock was created by students and teachers of Pavlovo Arts College in Russia and weighed 916 pounds.

417

Monday is named after the moon. Sunday is named after the sun.

418

The "French" in French fries actually refers to the style of slicing, known as "frenching," not the country.

419

The ancient Romans whitened their teeth using toothpaste made from human urine and goat milk.

420

In 1567, Hans Steininger, the man said to have the longest beard in the world died after he tripped over his beard running away from a fire.

421

The largest known living organism is an aspen grove in Utah nicknamed "Pando." The grove is a single organism that spans over 106 acres.

422

The longest English word is "pneumonoultramicroscopicsilicovolcanoconiosis," a type of lung disease caused by inhaling fine silicate or quartz dust.

423

Hailstones have been known to contain frogs and tadpoles.

424

Caesar salad is said to have been invented by Italian immigrant Caesar Cardini at his restaurant, Caesar's, in Tijuana, Mexico, on July 4, 1924.

425

An octopus has blue blood.

426

The shortest presidential term in U.S. history was William Henry Harrison's, lasting just 31 days.

427

Typewriter is the longest word that can be made using only the letters on one row of the keyboard.

428

There are more public libraries in the U.S. than McDonald's restaurants.

429

The longest time between two twins being born is 87 days.

430

The shortest theoretical physics paper ever published was Lander and Parkin's paper about a conjecture by Euleronly and was only two sentences long.

431

Lake Hillier in Australia is a bright pink color due to the presence of algae.

432

Edgar Allan Poe married his thirteen-year-old cousin.

433

There are more life forms living on your skin than there are people on the planet.

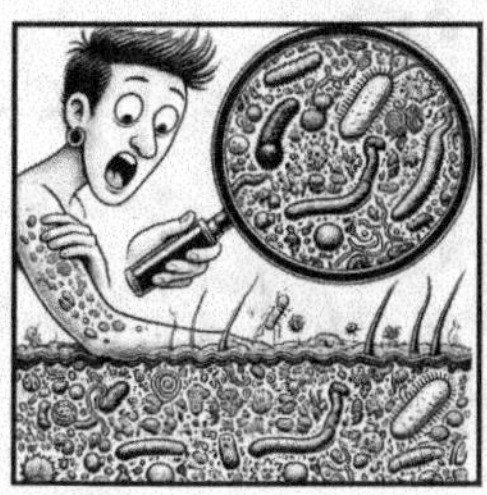

434

An adult human has fewer bones than a baby – some bones fuse together as growth occurs.

435

In ancient Egypt, people wore glittery cosmetics made from the crushed shells of beetles.

436

Goldfish can see infrared light.

437

If added together, humans
spend about two weeks of
their lifetimes kissing.

438

The inventor of the Pringles can now has
some of his ashes buried in one.

439

It's illegal to own just one guinea pig
in Switzerland because they are social
animals and get lonely.

440

Chocolate milk was
originally sold as a
medicine.

441

Al Capone's business card said he was a used furniture dealer.

442

Humans and giraffes have the same number of neck vertebrae.

443

The world's oldest piece of chewing gum is over 9,000 years old.

444

There are squares of chocolate that have less sugar than a slice of bread.

445

Saudi Arabia imports camels from Australia.

446

The first oranges weren't orange—they were green.

447

The first YouTube video was uploaded on April 23, 2005, and was called "Me at the zoo."

448

Facebook was originally named "TheFacebook".

449

Hot water will turn into ice faster than cold water, a phenomenon known as the "Mpemba effect".

450

The name of all the continents ends with the same letter that they start with.

451

There's a species of spider called the Hobo Spider.

452

A cockroach can live for a week without its head.

453

The banana cannot reproduce
itself. It can be propagated only
through cloning.

454

The jellyfish is 95 percent
water.

455

Prince Harry's official first
name is "Henry".

456

In the 16th century,
Turkish women could
initiate a divorce if their
husbands didn't pour
coffee for them.

457

Baseball was the sport featured on the first curved U.S. coin in 2014.

458

The inventor of the nacho was a man named Ignacio "Nacho" Anaya, who created the dish in 1943 in Mexico.

459

Cleopatra was not Egyptian - she was Greek.

460

The largest known meteorite weighs 60 tons and is located in Namibia.

461

'Bumbershoot' is another word for umbrella.

462

In New York City in 1962, Traffic Commissioner Henry Barnes implemented a short-lived traffic management system that required cars to stop at both cross-streets and intersections to allow pedestrians to cross diagonally from corner to corner. The confusion that ensued was called the "Barnes Dance."

463

There are 32 muscles in a cat's ear.

464

A group of porcupines is called a "prickle".

465

The first computer virus to be widely detected in the wild was Elk Cloner, created in 1982 by 15-year-old high school student Richard Skrenta.

466

The inventor of the light bulb, Thomas Edison, was afraid of the dark.

467

The shortest Grammy Award-winning song is "Stay" by Maurice Williams and the Zodiacs, which lasts just 1 minute and 37 seconds.

468

Galloping crocodiles inhabited the Sahara Desert 100 million years ago.

469

The shortest U.S. President was James Madison, standing at 5 feet 4 inches. The tallest was Abraham Lincoln, standing at 6 feet 4 inches.

470

The only letter that doesn't appear in any U.S. state name is "Q.'

471

472

In ancient Rome, uncooked barley soaked with wine was served as a staple breakfast.

473

The longest English word
without repeating any letter is
"uncopyrightable."

474

The world's largest ketchup bottle is a
170-foot tall water tower in Collinsville,
Illinois, built in 1949.

475

The "hashtag" symbol is technically
called an octothorpe. The octothorpe is
believed to have been adopted by the
telecommunications industry with the
advent of touch-tone dialing in the 1960s.

476

The shortest complete
sentence in English is "Go."

477

Riding roller coasters
can help you pass
kidney stones.

478

The inventor of the modern zipper,
Gideon Sundback, originally called it a
'separable fastener' when he improved
its design in 1913.

479

A shark is the only fish that
can blink with both eyes.

480

A "jiffy" is an actual unit of time:
1/100th of a second.

481

There is an official "Wizard of New Zealand." He has been an appointed position since 1990.

482

It's impossible to tickle yourself.

483

Frank Sinatra was offered the starring role in Die Hard when he was in his 70s.

484

The coldest inhabited place on Earth is Oymyakon, Russia, where temperatures can drop below -58 degrees Fahrenheit.

485

A bolt of lightning contains enough energy to toast 100,000 slices of bread.

486

The original name of the city of Bangkok, "Krung Thep Mahanakhon Amon Rattanakosin Mahinthara Ayuthaya Mahadilok Phop Noppharat Ratchathani Burirom Udomratchaniwet Mahasathan Amon Piman Awatan Sathit Sakkathattiya Witsanukam Prasit," is one of the longest place names in the world.

487

There are more stars in space than there are grains of sand on every beach in the world.

488

Quebec City is the only walled city in North America north of Mexico.

489

The heart of a blue whale is so large that a small child can swim through the arteries.

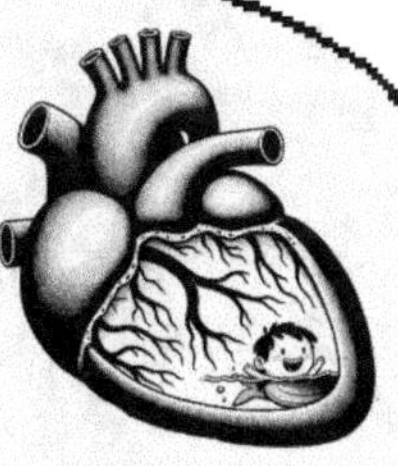

490

Venus rotates on its axis in the opposite direction to its orbit around the Sun.

491

There is a metallic asteroid shaped like a dog bone named "Kleopatra."

492

The Statue of Liberty is estimated to get struck by lightning at least 600 times per year.

493

There are about the same number of stars in the observable universe as there are grains of sand on all of Earth's beaches.

494

The fear of fun is called "cherophobia".

495

The shortest poem ever written is "Lines on the Antiquity of Microbes," also known simply as "Fleas," which reads: "Adam / Had'em."

496

Of all animals, snakes are the most sensitive to earthquakes.

497

Crocodiles can't stick out
their tongues.

498

Slugs have four noses.

499

A group of frogs is
called an "army".

500

There are 293 ways to make
change for a dollar.

501

Basenji dogs are the only breed that doesn't bark (they "yodel").

502

It is illegal to climb trees in Oshawa, a town in Ontario, Canada. The Canadian Law Discussion discusses the laws origins, "This law was put into place to prevent unable citizens from trying to act like Spiderman."

503

A group of larks is called an "exaltation", a "bevy", an "ascension" or a "happiness".

504

Alfred Porter Southwick (1826-1898), a dentist and professor at the University of Buffalo School of Dental Medicine, invented the electric chair.

Dear Trivia Buff,

We hope you enjoyed these random bits of trivia and that they brought a smile to your face or sparked a conversation. This collection was a labor of love, and we are grateful for your interest and support. Trivia is more than just facts; it's a celebration of curiosity and the joy of learning something new.

We would really appreciate a review from you. Thank you for being a part of this journey.

Stay curious!

Emma Fox

www.ingramcontent.com/pod-product-compliance
Lightning Source LLC
Chambersburg PA
CBHW061052250726